To: _____

From: _____

Date: _____

ONE PRAYER AWAY

Healing Words to Speak Over Your Day

Lauren Fortenberry

ZONDERVAN®

ZONDERVAN

One Prayer Away

© 2024 Lauren Fortenberry

Published in Grand Rapids, Michigan, by Zondervan. Zondervan is a registered trademark of The Zondervan Corporation, L.L.C., a wholly owned subsidiary of HarperCollins Christian Publishing, Inc.

Requests for information should be addressed to customercare@harpercollins.com.

ISBN 978-0-3104-6435-8 (audiobook)
ISBN 978-0-3104-6431-0 (eBook)
ISBN 978-0-3104-6433-4 (HC)

Image credits: Dima Zaharia/Shutterstock, page 11; Radharani/Shutterstock, page 19; Nomad_Soul/Shutterstock, page 27; Bogdan Sonjachnyj/Shutterstock, page 33; pixie_mfr/Shutterstock, page 49; Julia Pavaliuk/Shutterstock, page 57; Bogdan Sonjachnyj/Shutterstock, page 65; svetograph/Shutterstock, page 71; Karkhut/Shutterstock, page 89; Bogdan Sonjachnyj/Shutterstock, page 97; Bogdan Sonjachnyj/Shutterstock, page 105; Bogdan Sonjachnyj/Shutterstock, page 111; Bogdan Sonjachnyj/Shutterstock, page 127; Peera_stockfoto/Shutterstock, page 135; sgstudio/Shutterstock, page 143; roman.osinski/Shutterstock, page 149; Priscila Goodall/Shutterstock, page 167; Bogdan Sonjachnyj/Shutterstock, page 175; Bogdan Sonjachnyj/Shutterstock, page 183; pixie_mfr/Shutterstock, page 189; Erin Austen Abbott, page 200.

Art direction: Sabryna Lugge

Printed in Malaysia

24 25 26 27 28 VIV 10 9 8 7 6 5 4 3 2 1

To Mom—
For sowing the seeds of a saving faith.

To Aspen and Jansen—
For reminding me that love conquers all.

And to every woman still holding on.

CONTENTS

INTRODUCTION

Some time ago, I came across writing advice that I will never forget: *the best person you can write for is the person you were five years ago.* And, if I am honest, the year I turned thirty-three was the most difficult of my life. My father was diagnosed with stage 4 lung cancer, and our family was enduring a difficult season in the first weeks of that year. But in the deepest pit of my life, God did the unthinkable: He joined me.

Over the course of three months, I endured overwhelming grief and multiple eight-hour drives home to see my father while balancing full-time work and caring for two small children in a home where peace and rest were impossible for my heart to find. But God met me one day in my bedroom closet as I rediscovered a study Bible I had purchased a few months before. Every morning I woke up early, crawled into my closet, and talked to God through tears as I encountered His Word.

During that season, I remember searching online for *any* book that could speak to my situation: Grief. Loss. Trauma. Apart from the Bible, I was unable to find the right book for my circumstances. What I could not see then was that God was crafting this very book that you are reading now. So I have written this book for the person I was five years ago—and for you. God *knew* you would need this book for the journey ahead. This thought alone gives me chills and affirms a single truth for me: "You, LORD, keep my lamp burning; my God turns my darkness into light" (Psalm 18:28). Wherever you find yourself in this moment, God has a plan for your story, and He wants to lead you to His Light.

During the next ninety days, I want your life to be transformed through a closer walk with God—one that finally, *finally* surrenders to Him the heavy things you hold in your heart. Each day, you will read a devotion paired with an inspiring Bible verse and prayer to strengthen you where you are in your journey. My hope is that you will be spiritually fueled as God fills you with His peace and understanding. God loves you unconditionally, and this daily communion with Him will help you trust in His steadfast promises. Of course, some prayers and passages may bring someone else to mind, and you may want to share them and shine a light into their darkness! My heart is for all women to be lifted up in prayer and encouraged in their faith as they seek true healing in God.

To that end, this book is divided into three parts that focus on moving you from a broken beginning to a faith-filled future, while keeping you encouraged during the messy middle. No journey is linear, however, so every devotion has been crafted to lift your heart exactly where you are. More than anything, this book will cultivate a commitment to growing with God, even as the challenges of life come your way. You will walk with God in these next ninety days to overcome anxiety and overwhelm, to secure strength and direction, and to pursue life with God's peace and promises. The reflections and prayers included here will not help you bypass the burdens or hurry the healing, but they will steady your heart for a real and lasting relationship with God. Each day, your trust in Him will grow as you release a little more of what you carry.

My favorite verse in the Bible—the one God anchored to my soul years ago—is the promise that God also offers to you: "Then you will know the truth, and the truth will set you free" (John 8:32). You were not made to be wrapped up in worry. You were not made to fit back into the boxes you have outgrown. You were made to live free in God's Truth and Light.

When you are ready, confidently turn this page. God is ready. Let's faithfully go.

PART ONE

When the Beginning Is Broken

DEAR SISTER,

I am proud of you for being here, and I am proud of you for showing up. When things fall apart in our lives, our first response is often to run in the opposite direction. Presence is just too painful.

But I want to encourage you to start right here—where the beginning is broken.

You do not have to bear it alone.

In each of these devotions, I pray you will make room in your heart for God to join you. He wants to hear about your hurts. He wants to learn what keeps you up at night.

And He wants to heal it all.

Do not let the weight of the pieces you hold discourage you. God loves you. God is ready to make you whole.

Big hugs,

Lauren

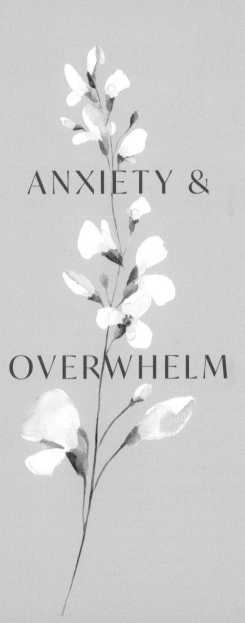

ANXIETY &

OVERWHELM

YOU ARE ONE PRAYER AWAY FROM A NEW LIFE

It sounds unbelievable until it happens.

You pray the impossible prayer.

Because you are at the edge of what your heart can handle.

You are at the edge of what your emotions can endure.

And even though you may have prayed that prayer many times before, this time is different.

Because something shifts on the outside.

God answers the prayer.
God opens the door.

And God invites you to take the next step into a whole new life.

This is the miracle of mercy.
This is the foundation of faith.

So today, offer that bold prayer with this sweet confidence:

One single prayer can change everything.

Because one single prayer can change *you*.

The prayer of a righteous person is powerful and effective.
JAMES 5:16

Dear God,

I pray for the woman who cannot see the road ahead.

Lord, her vision is clouded by emotions and overwhelming

uncertainty. Remind her, Father, that You will equip

her for every difficulty and decision—that You will be

beside her all the way. In Your Holy Name, Amen.

GOD KNOWS WHAT YOU FACE

It is tempting to believe that following God's will can prevent the storms.

The gut-wrenching heartache.
The broken relationships.
The devastating losses.

But trusting God is not about prevention.

It is about holy protection.

He knows what you face.
He understands what you face.

And He will hold you through it all.

Because the important work you were made to do does not happen in the absence of troubles.

But as a result of how you grow with God through them.

In every trial, cling to Him.

Because God is the Father who always watches.

And you are forever safe in His arms.

> Whoever dwells in the shelter of the Most High
> will rest in the shadow of the Almighty.
>
> PSALM 91:1–2

Dear God,

I pray for the woman who is waiting on You. Lord,

she has run to You in prayer, and she is so tired from

the struggle. Remind her, Father, that You hear every

cry, and Your power will be perfectly timed. Help her

lean into deeper trust. In Your Holy Name, Amen.

GIVE THE BROKEN TO GOD

You may be carrying something that you want to give to God, but you do not know how.

Because broken pieces are the heaviest of all.

Giving them to God admits something raw and uncomfortable.

And this vulnerable surrender can lead you to feel guilt and shame.

It is far easier to ignore your hidden truth than to acknowledge it.

But God invites you with love:

I know it hurts. I know it will continue to hurt. But I am the Healer.

So take the next small step in turning over to God what makes your thoughts and soul uneasy.

Because God does not just hold the remedy.

But the restoration of every wound.

By His grace.
In His mercy.

Through His unending love.

When anxiety was great within me, your consolation brought me joy.
PSALM 94:19

Dear God,

I pray for the woman who is living inside of the

hurt. Lord, it is all she can feel and think about—no

matter how hard she tries. Remind her, Father, that

You will bring freedom to her heart and that every

prayer is protection. In Your Holy Name, Amen.

WHEN ANXIETY IS GREAT, GOD'S LOVE IS GREATER

When worry and anxious thoughts come, they seem to want to permanently stay.

To disrupt your thoughts.
To distract you from your purpose.

But the truth that can free your heart is this: God's love is greater.

He will not allow you to be consumed by the waves or the fire.

And He whispers: *I am with You.*

In a world where everything changes and nothing stays the same, His promise is the only one upon which you can rely.

Today, let your heart lean on His love.

And the relentless threat of anxiety.

Will fade. Will fade. *Will fade.*

Do not be anxious about anything.
PHILIPPIANS 4:6

Dear God, I pray for the woman who feels like a prisoner to her anxiety. Lord, just when she feels free and in control, her thoughts take her captive. Remind her, Father, that You will not leave her in the dark—that Your love will break down every wall to her heart's peace. In Your Holy Name, Amen.

day 5

WHEN LIFE IS SHAKEN,
IT CAN BE SHAPED BY GOD

Faith is not about calm seas or blue skies.

It is about feeling the boat shake.

Not because God wants to stir up drama in your life.

But because He wants to stir up revival in your heart.

And when you grip the sides of the boat.

He is inviting you to growth.
He is calling you to a life of more.

Because He is still in control.

Whether you are in the storm now or will inevitably face one to come.

Let this comforting truth surround you:

The One who made the skies, the seas, and the storms will sustain you to the other side.

> The LORD is my strength and my shield; my
> heart trusts in him, and he helps me.
> PSALM 28:7

Dear God,

I pray for the woman who is doing her best to make it through. Lord, it feels like she has given all of herself, but the challenges keep coming. Remind her, Father, that You will take over when her heart is weary, and she can trust that her future will be filled with Your enduring love. In Your Holy Name, Amen.

GOD CAN HOLD THE HEAVY

The longer you carry the baggage, the more it weighs you down.

It holds you back from hope, and it distances you from God's holy destination for your life.

Still, you cling to the heavy.

Because you get scared.
Because you get overwhelmed.

Because you forget that God controls it all.

But remember this: letting go is a process.

It takes prayer.
It takes persistence.

And it requires a complete surrender of pride.

You cannot do it.

But He *can*.

If you find yourself unable to hold on but unable to let go, trust in this promise:

In God's mighty hands, the heavy can be healed.

> His splendor was like the sunrise; rays flashed from
> his hand, where his power was hidden.
> HABAKKUK 3:4

Dear God,

I pray for the woman who is trusting You with

something big. Lord, she has carried it to Your feet,

and she is feeling every emotion. Remind her, Father,

that the One who made the mountains will help her

climb every single one. In Your Holy Name, Amen.

GOD CAN REDEEM WHAT YOU GIVE HIM

Sometimes surrender feels like giving up.

You have messes that cannot be cleaned.

Pieces that will not go back together.

It all feels hopeless.

So you trust the broken to God.

And, often, it takes everything within you to hand it over.

Because you think you can fix things yourself.
Because you ignore handling what you would rather avoid.

And you forget the most simple truth:

God will redeem.

Because He cares.
Because He loves.

Because only He knows what is best for you.

In the release of what you cannot reconcile, know this:

God's redemption is on the way.

> Israel, put your hope in the LORD, for with the LORD is
> unfailing love and with him is full redemption.
> PSALM 130:7

Dear God,

I pray for the woman who wants to believe that good

things are ahead. Lord, she has held onto hope before,

but disappointment nearly destroyed her. Remind her,

Father, that You are with her in the valley and Your voice

will lead her to the light. In Your Holy Name, Amen.

GOD WILL HOLD YOU TOGETHER

In the hardest seasons of life, sometimes the only thing that can save you is surrender.

A simple trust that God will hold together all the parts of you that have come undone.

You may be wrapped up in denial and distraction.

Maybe you have been for years.

But the incredible thing is God waits for you.

In the cracking.
In the breaking.

Until the desperate prayers you offer become the very foundation upon which your faith is built.

Today, let your life fall into His able hands.

Because the Maker of all things is also the Mender.

He heals the brokenhearted and binds up their wounds.

PSALM 147:3

Dear God, I pray for the woman who feels like things are falling apart. Lord, she has spent so many hours and so much of her energy trying to keep life together, but she feels defeated. Remind her, Father, that what is broken will be healed in Your hands. In Your Holy Name, Amen.

*A*nd she learned to trust in all
the details she could not see.

God was working.

God was perfectly timing
every promise.

GOD IS WORKING IT OUT

There are times when you feel like the world is falling apart and the rug has been pulled from beneath you.

But this is not God's punishment or rejection.

This is the Almighty preserving your very life.

The boat is going to rock. The ground is going to quake.

But this is not the death of your hope.

It is the resurrection of your future.

God is waking you up.
God is holding you close to His chest.

And God is preparing you for victory.

Where His name is glorified.
When His purposes are fulfilled.

And all the messes of today become your mission for tomorrow.

God is working it out.

Because God never stops working in *you*.

> For it is God who works in you to will and to
> act in order to fulfill his good purpose.
> PHILIPPIANS 2:13

Dear God,

I pray for the woman who is trying to let go of what

she cannot control. Lord, her heart is hurting, and she

is struggling to release the future to You. Remind her,

Father, that on the other side of the worry and waiting

is Your precious peace. In Your Holy Name, Amen.

LEAN ON GOD'S STRENGTH

There will be days when you struggle to get out of bed.

But you can lean on God's strength.

There will be moments where you feel depressed and numb.

But you can lean on God's strength.

And there will be situations where you feel completely overwhelmed.

But you can lean on God's strength.

Because His promise is not that He will be with you or help you once.

But *always*.

Every time.
Every circumstance.

Today, let this promise offer hope:

No matter the burden. No matter what you bear.

God is strong enough to endure all you bring with you.

Lean on Him.
Lean on His unchanging love.

> The LORD, the LORD himself, is my strength and
> my defense; he has become my salvation.
>
> ISAIAH 12:2

Dear God,

I pray for the woman who does not know how much longer

she can hold on. Lord, she has done what she can, and all

she has left is trust. But she is slipping. Remind her, Father,

that when she loses hope, Your arms will reach for her

until her heart rises to You. In Your Holy Name, Amen.

TRUST GOD WITH EVERYTHING

It seems simple enough, giving it all to God.

But the truth is, releasing it all means you also must confess:

You are not in control.

That feels scary and impossible.

But in your moment of greatest surrender.

God fills the insecurities.
God quiets the fears.

And God helps you take the next right step in faith.

Only when you take your hands off the hard can God make what comes next holy.

> Trust in him at all times, you people; pour out
> your hearts to him, for God is our refuge.
> PSALM 62:8

Dear God,

I pray for the woman who wants to release her fear.

Lord, she has tried to let it go, but it clings to every

thought and leaves her afraid to move. Remind her,

Father, that Your love can drive out the lies and lead

her to a life of hope. In Your Holy Name, Amen.

GOD CAN STILL MAKE IT BEAUTIFUL

It is the situation you do not want to talk about.

The one that threatens your peace.
The one that tests your faith.

And it just seems to get worse, not better.

But your trial will never be beyond God's reach and redemption.

There is still a way for God to move here.
There is still time for God to make it beautiful.

Today, let this truth strengthen each prayer that flows:

God knows your every hurt.

And God can heal every broken thing.

> He has made everything beautiful in its time.
> ECCLESIASTES 3:11

Dear God, I pray for the woman who is struggling to trust her healing to the Healer. Lord, she knows You have not abandoned her, but this situation feels too far gone. Remind her, Father, that Your love is never late and Your redemption is never out of reach. In Your Holy Name, Amen.

And she had faith that this season
would not last forever.

God was holding her hand.

God was preparing her peace.

God was strengthening her soul.

GOD WILL GIVE YOUR HEART
THE STRENGTH TO SING

When you are in the midst of hardship and struggle, it does not feel like joy will ever be possible again.

You lose the ability to look around and savor what is.

You do your best just to make it through.

Faith, however, teaches us that God did not make our hearts to simply survive.

But to *sing*.

Even when we do not see the good.
Even when we do not feel the good.

Deep within us we know that God is good, and He will strengthen us to hold onto hope.

Because the God who helps us endure is the same God who will lead us to enjoy.

Cling to Him tightly.

And He will grow your gladness.

I will pray with my spirit, but I will also pray with my understanding;
I will sing with my spirit, but I will also sing with my understanding.
1 CORINTHIANS 14:15

Dear God,

I pray for the woman whose heart is aching. Lord,

the hurt is multilayered, and it comes to her without

warning. Remind her, Father, that this season will not

last forever, and where there is darkness Your light is

always on the way. In Your Holy Name, Amen.

GOD WAITS FOR YOU WITH OPEN ARMS

It is impossible to know what you are carrying.

In your life.
In your arms.
In your heart.

But God waits for you with open arms.

Because He loves and cares for you.
Because He did not design you to hold it all.

And surrender is not just giving it to God.

It is also trusting that He will bless the broken—trusting that He will make miracles from life's greatest messes.

Today, may your heart be blessed by this single truth:

God wants to resolve what you cannot reconcile.

So that you can rest.
So that you can be restored.

God is able.

He is waiting.

> The eternal God is your refuge, and
> underneath are the everlasting arms.
> DEUTERONOMY 33:27

Dear God,

I pray for the woman whose heart is heavy. Lord, she is

filled with anxiety and every emotion, and she cannot

seem to let any of it go. Remind her, Father, that she

can trust You with her baggage, and Your mercy will

lighten her story and soul. In Your Holy Name, Amen.

IN THE DEEPEST WATERS, GOD WILL BE WITH YOU

The hardest times in life are when you feel most alone.

When you feel deserted.
When you feel rejected.

When you are left without hope.

But God whispers this promise for every problem:

I am here. I am with you. Do not fear.

If your heart and eyes are aligned with God, you can trust in Him.

There is no quick and easy.

But there is possible with God.

For in the deepest waters, He will be with you.

And on the darkest days, He will never stop leading you to the Light.

When you pass through the waters, I will be with you.
ISAIAH 43:2

Dear God, I pray for the woman who is trying to survive this season. Lord, it has all become too much, but she is still moving. Remind her, Father, that You built her heart to endure and You will lead her through every darkness. In Your Holy Name, Amen.

*A*nd she did not have to
have it all figured out
before she could get started.

She prayed.
She trusted.

And God helped her begin.

GOD CAN USE IT FOR GOOD

The relationships that don't work out.
The dreams that remain unfulfilled.
The losses that take your very breath away.

These are all things that God can use for good.

In His way. In His time.

He does not leave you without.

He strengthens you. He sustains you.

And, in your faith, He makes you a brand-new creation.

Take heart.

Because in the disappointment and grief, God's love is working.

It will chase you down.
It will hold you up.

It will remind you that He has a plan.

Because life is not the story of what you can do.

But what God can do through you.

And He is just getting started.

> He is the Rock, his works are perfect, and all his ways are just.
> DEUTERONOMY 32:4

Dear God,

I pray for the woman who wants to believe the healing

will come. Lord, she knows that forgiveness will be

hard, but nothing is out of reach for You. Remind

her, Father, that You hold redemption and revival in

Your merciful hands. In Your Holy Name, Amen.

GOD MAKES DREAMS FROM DUST

The situation seems hopeless.

There is no redeeming or rescue.

That is, until God steps in.

He sweeps together the dust.

And He makes meaning from the mess.

The lost causes are no longer lost.
The failed attempts are no longer failures.

For when you wholly lean on the God of the universe, you will see the resurrection of the dreams He spoke into your heart.

Because God has not abandoned His mission.

He is still working.
He is still moving.

And there is no corner of your life that God will leave dead or deserted.

For in the waiting, your Father whispers:

Just wait, child. Just wait.

> The LORD has compassion on those who fear him; for he knows how we are formed, he remembers that we are dust.
>
> PSALM 103:13–14

Dear God,

I pray for the woman who finds herself standing in the

ashes. Lord, the journey has been long and painful,

and she is struggling to sustain her strength. Remind

her, Father, that You can still make beautiful things

with broken dreams. In Your Holy Name, Amen.

WITH GOD, OVERWHELM CAN BE OVERCOME

Just when you think you have things figured out, overwhelm begins to manifest in a new way.

For the problems you cannot solve.
For the feelings you cannot reconcile.

And the anxiety can be crippling.

Until you remember God's promise:

I am with you always. Even to the very end.

And you begin to realize that this is not just a fleeting, one-time promise.

But an "every day I will help you get out of bed" promise.

Because God gets it.
Because God gets *you*.

He will equip you with the tools to not only survive the overwhelm.

But to overcome life's greatest adversities.

And one day, you will get to share the story:

In your broken places.

God made you whole.

And surely I am with you always, to the very end of the age.
Matthew 28:20

Dear God,

I pray for the woman who feels like the mountain cannot

be moved. Lord, she has prayed for change for so long

that it feels impossible. Remind her, Father, that behind

the scenes You are working, and Your strength alone will

carry her to the other side. In Your Holy Name, Amen.

STRENGTH &

DIRECTION

GOD HAS NOT FORGOTTEN YOUR STRUGGLES

When you try to navigate the hardest parts of life, the Enemy will try to convince you:

God is not listening.

And, you must admit, it is tempting to buy into.

Because your prayer is not magically answered.

Because you can see no evidence of God working on your behalf.

Still, everything you have survived tells you He is there.

The doors He closed.
The people He removed.

The path that could have been carved only by Him.

So you bravely choose to believe He cares—that He has not forgotten what you are enduring.

Because over and over faith reveals:

God is not in the business of rejection, but resurrection.

And every single cry and concern you leave at His feet?

They help you learn to trust Him a little more.

> But as for me, I watch in hope for the LORD, I wait
> for God my Savior; my God will hear me.
> MICAH 7:7

Dear God,

I pray for the woman who worries she will never

get there. Lord, she prays and gives her best, but life

adds more obstacles each day. Remind her, Father,

that You will strengthen her heart to hope and persist

with purpose. In Your Holy Name, Amen.

SHOW UP IN FAITH

You spend your days looking for an invitation.

For signs.
For circumstances.

Something that points to God being ready to use you.

But the truth is, He has been there all along.

Waiting for you to show up for His directions in faith.

Because when God breathed life into you, it was by design.

To complete His good works.
To carry out His amazing plans.

And to confess that God is King of your heart every step of the way.

So lean into the uncertainty and unknown with this truth:

God will use you.

God will bless others through your life.

> And without faith it is impossible to please God, because
> anyone who comes to him must believe that he exists
> and that he rewards those who earnestly seek him.
> HEBREWS 11:6

Dear God,

I pray for the woman who is gathering her strength.

Lord, life has pushed her down and the world has

pushed her around, but she does not quit. Remind her,

Father, that You will equip her and sustain her for

every battle ahead. In Your Holy Name, Amen.

YOUR CALLING WILL NEVER COME FROM THE WORLD

You are not called to convince other people of your calling.

And you are not called to make sure the world understands what God has uniquely made you to do.

Your one job is to follow after Him with your whole heart.

Not just a little.
Not just when it is convenient.

Going all in:

Mind. Body. Soul.

But if you are a people pleaser, the temptation to detour and perform will abound.

Today, let your heart rest in this truth:

The calling comes from within.

Listen to it. Let it guide you.

And no matter the worldly adversity:

Love God with *all* you have.

> Each person should live as a believer in whatever
> situation the Lord has assigned to them.
>
> 1 CORINTHIANS 7:17

Dear God,

I pray for the woman who is being prepared for big things.

Lord, she feels You leading her, but she so easily loses

confidence and questions Your ways. Remind her, Father, that

You are not giving up on her—even if her heart pauses, even

if her foot steps off the path. In Your Holy Name, Amen.

THE ENEMY WANTS YOU TO QUIT

When it is hard to get out of bed.
When it is impossible to keep going.

The Enemy wants you to abandon all hope.

It feels like the ship is sinking.

And you will too.

But in your time of greatest discouragement, God is there with you.

He invites you to rest.

Not with candles and bubble baths.

But in the sense that finally, *finally* you can let things go and believe that God is in control.

In the release, He will give you the strength to survive.

And the peace to endure every tough day you will face.

Be still, and know that I am God.
PSALM 46:10

Dear God, I pray for the woman who is trying to rest in You. Lord, she knows she cannot do it all, but she still tries anyway. And she is exhausted. Remind her, Father, that what she places in Your hands will never be broken but blessed. In Your Holy Name, Amen.

And she learned to take it
one day at a time,
one step at a time,
one breath at a time.

God would be with her all the way.

GOD IS NOT PULLING YOU AWAY
FROM GOOD THINGS

Before you gave your whole life to Christ, you always felt this pulling.

God tugging you away from the world and toward Him.

You used to think it was because you were falling short of His dream for your life.

You felt shame, guilt, and all the ingredients that make self-loathing.

You even tried to run away.

But what you did not realize was this truth:

No amount of running makes God chase you any less.

Eventually, you must surrender.

Because your heart was made for more.

Only God knows the way.

And with every single prayer.

You become a little more whole.

> Consider it pure joy, my brothers and sisters, whenever
> you face trials of many kinds, because you know that
> the testing of your faith produces perseverance.
>
> JAMES 1:2–4

Dear God,

I pray for the woman who is ready to live in Your truth. Lord,

she has made excuses and has hidden from the hard, but she

knows it is time to face forward. Remind her, Father, that

You will surround her with grace, and You will shepherd

every day ahead with love. In Your Holy Name, Amen.

IN THE WAITING, GOD IS PREPARING

You like to see what is ahead.

When you are driving.
When you are planning.

And when you are preparing.

But faith strips that comfort away.

Because you have to trust that God has the answers.

That He alone can see the road ahead.

And you are called to follow.

Sometimes, you will feel lost. But trust God anyway.

Sometimes, you will feel scared. But trust God anyway.

Without fail, He will shift something in you as you cling to His promises and wait.

He will refocus your heart on what is important.
He will strengthen your will in every step.

Because the waiting? It is never easy.

But God's love? It never, ever wavers.

> Maintain love and justice, and wait for your God always.
> HOSEA 12:6

Dear God,

I pray for the woman who is trusting that You will

open the door. Lord, she has felt You walk this journey

with her, but her faith needs a nudge to keep going.

Remind her, Father, that You are leading her to where

hope becomes healing. In Your Holy Name, Amen.

TRUSTING GOD ANCHORS YOUR HEART TO HOPE

All it takes is a little uncomfortable uncertainty to shake your faith.

To make you question God.
To make you question following after Him.

But you really have two options:

Abandon the faith you have grown.
Or cling tighter to your hope.

Because the truth is, uncertainty gives you what you need to grow.

No, you may not like or want it.

But every time you choose to embrace God in the chaos of life,
you have this Anchor.

And it allows your roots to grow.

Today, lean in and trust a little deeper.

God is leading.

God still knows the way.

> The LORD gives strength to his people; the
> LORD blesses his people with peace.
> PSALM 29:11

Dear God,

I pray for the woman who is clinging to You. Lord,

her heart feels tugged and tested, but her fingers are

holding on to You tightly. Remind her, Father, that Your

truth will free her and Your love will strengthen her to

keep trusting in You. In Your Holy Name, Amen.

GOD WILL LEAD YOU DOWN
THE PATH HE MADE FOR YOU

You used to spend your time looking around.

To make sure you were measuring up.
To make sure you were keeping up.

Because your heart did not know the most healing truth:

You are not supposed to run anyone else's race.

For God equips each person with gifts that others do not have.

So today, let not concern but confidence enter in.

Let there be no more comparison.

But compassion for your soul.

God is ready to walk the unknown and uncertain paths ahead with you.

Let His love encourage every single step.

If I were still trying to please people, I would not be a servant of Christ.
GALATIANS 1:10

Dear God, I pray for the woman who is trying to make hard changes. Lord, the mountain she hopes to climb is steep, but she is following Your footsteps. Remind her, Father, that there is no failure in faith and You will hold her through every fear. In Your Holy Name, Amen.

And she could do hard things.

Not by her own strength.

But by God's.

He would carry her
through every impossible day.

day 27

GOD WILL REPLACE YOUR STRESS WITH STRENGTH

It is difficult to give to God what you carry.

In your arms.
In your heart.

And the stress can build and build.

But if you can hold on to hope while letting go of your fears and frustrations.

God can do the work.

And not just out there in the world.

But deep inside of you too.

Because what God allows can grow your strength.

If you let Him have His way.
If you trust that God's plan is best.

He will help you rise and face what comes next.

Because He *knows*.

Because He wants to prepare you today.

> So do not fear, for I am with you; do not be dismayed,
> for I am your God. I will strengthen you and help you;
> I will uphold you with my righteous right hand.
>
> ISAIAH 41:10

Dear God,

I pray for the woman who is navigating intense stress. Lord,

it feels like she is carrying the world on her back and within

her heart. Remind her, Father, that You will give her the

strength to release it all—to rest in knowing that Your hands

never grow weak or weary. In Your Holy Name, Amen.

DO NOT GIVE UP BEFORE THE BLESSING

One of the more difficult parts of faith is holding on to God's plan when life says, "Give up."

When you face failure.
When you face rejection.

When it feels like losing is all but inevitable.

But God does not promise that you will be able to understand or explain to the world why you are doing it.

He promises to love and comfort you along the way. *His* way.

Following the holy calling He has breathed into your heart.

Keep enduring with this encouragement:

God put you on this path with purpose.

On the other side of the hard is the most healing knowledge of all:

You served God all the way.
He completed a beautiful work in you.

And you did not surrender the blessings.

You surrendered your life to the only One who can bestow them.

Be strong and do not give up, for your work will be rewarded.
2 CHRONICLES 15:7

Dear God,

I pray for the woman who is still showing up. Lord,

You see how big her giants are, but You also see the

size of her heart. Remind her, Father, that the battle

is Yours, and faith will give her the right tools at

exactly the right time. In Your Holy Name, Amen.

GOD WILL GIVE YOU THE STRENGTH

When you feel paralyzed and weighed down by the next step you know you must take.

It all feels like too much.

You want to give up.
You want to run and hide.

But God finds you there, and He whispers this steadfast promise:

I will give you strength.

Trust. Move. Believe.

And the once impossible hope and peace find their way into your heart.

Because God does not abandon you in the hard.

In fact, it is where He meets you.

Because you were never designed to endure life alone.

But to walk with your Waymaker.

Until the love that transcends all understanding.

Becomes the strength you need to overcome.

> Be strong and courageous. Do not be afraid or terrified
> because of them, for the LORD your God goes with you.
> DEUTERONOMY 31:6

Dear God,

I pray for the woman who has forgotten her strength. Lord,

she does not know how to fight the enemies she faces, and her

spirit is discouraged. Remind her, Father, that You will protect

her heart and preserve her life. In Your Holy Name, Amen.

GOD WILL SHOW YOU THE WAY

Life is really hard.

And sometimes you may not know what words to say or which way to go.

But God holds these answers in His faithful heart.

It takes relentless prayer to get glimpses of the right direction.

He gave you ears to listen and a heart to obey.

And He gave you feet to go to the places He has prepared.

The trusting, however, is the true leap.

When you are not sure if your faith is enough.
When you are not sure if He will catch you in the surrender.

But when you can overcome the overwhelm.

You will find the walk becomes the way becomes His wisdom.

> If any of you lacks wisdom, you should ask God, who
> gives generously . . . and it will be given to you.
> JAMES 1:5

Dear God, I pray for the woman who is desperate for Your direction. Lord, she has been listening for Your voice, but the time of decision has come. Remind her, Father, that You hold time and tomorrow in Your hands and You will come through. In Your Holy Name, Amen.

And she learned to pray
through the worst of life.

God would listen.

God would shower her with grace.

God would never leave
her without direction.

GOD WILL HOLD YOUR HAND THROUGH

Sometimes you may think there is a way to avoid life's troubles.

But the closer you walk with God, the more this truth illuminates:

The way is through.

This requires trusting God in every impossible step.

And sometimes, this is quite painful.

But in the unknown and overwhelming uncertainty:

He knows what you need. He knows how you will get there.

And He loves you no matter what your eyes see or where your feet land.

With His unending grace, you can make it to the other side.

Changed *forever*.

Because when life attacked you, you put on the armor of God.

To love others. To serve Him with your gifts.

And to show the world:

God will illuminate every step to the most abundant life you could ever hope to have.

> I am the LORD your God . . . who directs you.
> ISAIAH 48:17

Dear God,

I pray for the woman who knows she cannot stay where

she is. Lord, You have called her to more; she feels it,

and she believes it in her heart. Remind her, Father,

that her faith will guide her, and she will never be

lost with Your love. In Your Holy Name, Amen.

IF GOD CALLS YOU TO IT, NOTHING CAN KEEP YOU FROM IT

Fear and anxiety want you to believe a powerful lie:

You are going to miss God's blessing.

And something is going to keep you from where God is calling you.

But that is just not true.

Because God's way is unchanging.

So do not get wrapped up in the snares of blame and regret.

Let yourself get lost in God's grace.

Even when you cannot see it or feel it, God is preparing the path.

Keep chasing His light.
Focus on His steps alone.

And the peace that passes all understanding will find you.

It will confirm that our loving Lord has been with you all along.

> Whether you turn to the right or to the left, your ears will hear
> a voice behind you, saying, "This is the way; walk in it."
> ISAIAH 30:21

Dear God,

I pray for the woman who feels like she has missed her

boat. Lord, no matter how hard she tries or plans, she

cannot seem to keep life moving toward her highest

hopes. Remind her, Father, that You know every ache

of her heart, and You are forever faithful in where

You have called her. In Your Holy Name, Amen.

GOD WILL HELP YOU RISE

When you feel most defeated, that is when God is preparing your victory.

Not winning in the world's eyes.

But being victorious in the heart of God.

He sees your faithfulness.
He sees your righteousness.

And He is timing every good thing.

The darkness wants to confuse and cloud your vision.

But God is there.

So let the sun and His Son remind you:

Your rise is coming.

His redemption is making all things *new*.

Arise, shine, for your light has come.
ISAIAH 60:1

Dear God, I pray for the woman who wants to believe her best days are ahead. Lord, she has seen dark days, but her heart has held on. Remind her, Father, that where Your hope leads her is where Your hands have prepared good things. In Your Holy Name, Amen.

*A*nd she stopped longing
for what was or what
could have been.

God made no mistake
in leading her here.

And her pain would only
strengthen her purpose.

GOD WILL GROW YOU IN WHAT YOU GO THROUGH

When you face difficulties, it is easy to spend time in self-blame and frustration.

As if God is a God of punishment. Not love.

But pause and ask yourself this question:

What is God trying to grow in you?

Because you know that He has a plan.
Because you know that He has a purpose.

And the truth that can free your heart is this:

God wants the best for His children.

And what He leads you to is hope.

Even in the desert.
Even in the wilderness.

Because with God, you do not just go.

You *grow* through every trial.

> Just as you received Christ Jesus as Lord, continue to live your
> lives in him, rooted and built up in him, strengthened in the
> faith as you were taught, and overflowing with thankfulness.
>
> COLOSSIANS 2:6–7

Dear God,

I pray for the woman who is braving the wilderness.

Lord, this desert is unlike any she has faced, and her

soul is so thirsty. Remind her, Father, that You will

show up for her—that You will be her forever Guide

in the great unknown. In Your Holy Name, Amen.

day 35

THE MORE YOU LOOK FOR GOD,
THE MORE YOU WILL SEE HIM

When you look to the world, you can feel depressed.

But when you look to God, you will feel refreshed.

Because His way is truth and life and hope.

And you can only get there if your eyes are searching for Him.

Most often, you will find Him through prayer or His Word.

But sometimes it is a song.

Or a stranger who extends God's grace.

For when you see God, you see why you are here.

To love God. To love others.

To shine His light for always.

Today, let these words fill your soul:

The more you look for God, the more you will see Him in all of your life.

And the deepest peace will come.

> We know also that the Son of God has come and has
> given us understanding, so that we may know him who
> is true. . . . He is the true God and eternal life.
> I JOHN 5:20

Dear God,

I pray for the woman who is struggling to lift her eyes to

You. Lord, her days have been distressed and her hope has

been heavy, and she needs to remember Your love. Remind

her, Father, that You will strengthen her vision until she can

trust in Your perfect plan. In Your Holy Name, Amen.

GOD WAS THERE ALL ALONG WITH LOVE

Perhaps you used to think God was waiting on you to move.

That you had to get it right to get to Him.

But God is God.

And He waits for you with the purest love.

Not because of anything you have done to earn it.
But because of His unending mercy and grace.

Your job is simply to show up.

To open yourself to His will.
To release your fears and failures to Him.

And to trust that He waits for you there.

Today, let your life be inspired by a truth the world can never steal:

Nothing can separate you from God.

When you move your heart closer to Him, you invite God's love to change every moment ahead.

For His glory.
For your *good*.

The LORD is good to those whose hope is in
him, to the one who seeks him.
LAMENTATIONS 3:25

Dear God,

I pray for the woman who keeps going. Lord, she does not

know how she has made it this far, but she needs Your

strength to make it to the other side. Remind her, Father,

that You will lift her heart when it is weary, and You will fill

her when her spirit runs dry. In Your Holy Name, Amen.

PART TWO

When the Middle Is Messy

DEAR SISTER,

Can you feel it? You are walking closer to God with every prayer, and this intimacy with our Lord is leading to a revival in your heart. God is making things new and timing every promise.

But the middle is when your patience can begin to feel pressed.

You may even be asking yourself: *Why am I not there yet? Why is it taking so long?*

I want to encourage you to cling to your hope and faith, because the Enemy wants to tempt you with powerful lies. Stay steadfast in the middle of this journey, because God is strengthening your beautiful and precious heart.

And the healing that feels just out of reach?

It has already begun.

Big hugs,

Lauren

SELF-LOVE &

SELF-WORTH

YOU ARE FULLY KNOWN AND FULLY LOVED BY GOD

When the world takes a step back from you, God takes a step closer.

When the world makes you feel unworthy, God whispers, *You are valued.*

And when the world rejects who you are, God keeps the light shining in you.

Because the One who made the world is not of it.

He took the time to design every single part of you.

And He knows you fully.

So keep growing in Him.

No matter what.

Keep trusting in Him.

No matter what.

And keep your faith in His mighty way.

No matter what.

The LORD appeared to us in the past, saying: "I have loved you with an everlasting love; I have drawn you with unfailing kindness."

JEREMIAH 31:3

Dear God,

I pray for the woman who is fighting negative voices.

Lord, she has tried to ignore them, but they threaten

her peace. Remind her, Father, that no matter what

strength or progress these voices try to steal, Your

love can heal. In Your Holy Name, Amen.

GOD DID NOT MAKE YOU LIKE
ANYONE ELSE ON PURPOSE

Sometimes, you get really frustrated.

When you do not feel understood.
When you feel too different from others.

But let God speak peace gently into your heart:

I set you apart.

Your gifts were never made to fit into boxes or others' expectations.

No, God is far bigger than that.

Listen with all your heart to where He is calling you.

And you will not waste time in the "why" questions.

You will get right to work.

It does not matter what others say about you.
It does not matter what others do around you.

Keep listening to God.
Keep loving Him with all you have.

And the doors that need to be opened will open.

> Whoever gives heed to instruction prospers, and
> blessed is the one who trusts in the LORD.
>
> PROVERBS 16:20

Dear God,

I pray for the woman who has lost her confidence.

Lord, she used to walk with strength, but she finds

herself questioning and doubting. Remind her, Father,

that she can trust where You are leading, and the

healing will come. In Your Holy Name, Amen.

GOD CARES MORE ABOUT YOUR HEART THAN YOUR HUSTLE

The Enemy wants to keep you striving.

Because then you will stay distracted.
Because then you will be exhausted.

And God's unique call in your life will take a back seat.

Hope and healing, however, will never come through the hustle.

But through God working in your heart.

And only when your heart is aligned with Him will you experience the riches of life.

Purpose for your days and peace for your soul.

And the reminder that life is all about love.

Today, let these words comfort and challenge you:

Walk humbly with your God.

Do not hurry the hustle.
Run the race set before you.

And God will set the pace.

> And what does the LORD require of you? To act justly and
> to love mercy and to walk humbly with your God.
> MICAH 6:8

Dear God,

I pray for the woman who is burned out. Lord, she has loved

so hard that she has emptied herself of energy with endless

giving. Remind her, Father, that You did not create her to do

it all, but to carry it all to You. In Your Holy Name, Amen.

day 40

GOD HAS WRITTEN HIS NAME ON YOUR HEART

When you get scared.

When you fear the outcome.

Quiet your thoughts, and let God whisper a reminder:

My Name is on your heart.

I created you with love. I created you to live a life of love.

And you will feel your purpose return.

The world is determined to distract and deter.

But God alone can drive you to meaning.

Rest in this peace:

You can never lose God.
You can always find direction in your Creator.

> For from him and through him and for him are
> all things. To him be the glory forever!
> ROMANS 11:36

Dear God, I pray for the woman who needs to hear Your voice over all the others. Lord, her world is filled with opinions and noise, and she seeks You alone. Remind her, Father, that You have come so that she might have life. Please guide her along the path with grace. In Your Holy Name, Amen.

And nd she did not give up.

Even when it got hard.
Even when it got heavy.

Because God's love never left her.

GOD IS SO PROUD OF YOU

When you have worked hard with your whole heart, and no one notices or cares.

God is so proud of you.

When you have broken impossible cycles and are still standing, and no one notices or cares.

God is so proud of you.

And when you are no longer the person who is afraid and tries to stay small, and no one notices or cares.

God is so proud of you.

Because He is the only One who sees the whole picture.

Every battle. Every scar.

Every single ounce of growth.

When the journey feels lonely, remember that you are loved by a faithful God.

When every single voice is silent, remember that God is cheering for you.

He is your *biggest* fan.

> How precious to me are your thoughts, God!
> How vast is the sum of them!
> PSALM 139:17

Dear God,

I pray for the woman who has been hard on herself.

Lord, she has big goals, but she cannot seem to get closer

to them—no matter how much she tries. Remind her,

Father, that the path You have made for her cannot be

missed or messed up. In Your Holy Name, Amen.

WHAT GOD HAS FOR YOU
CANNOT BE STOLEN OR LOST

There is a lie that anxiety whispers over and over to your heart:

"You will never get there."

Because you are not good enough.
Because you will always miss the mark.

But that is not true of God's grace or love.

He will not reassign His blessings or allow someone to steal them away.

And you can find your way back once you know:

It is not about perfection.
It is not about a problem-free life.

It is about learning to trust that nothing can keep you from God's plan.

Let these words reassure your soul:

You do not have to hustle or rush or stress.
You can rest in the surrender.

And wait with faith on His faithfulness.

> The Lord is not slow in keeping his promise, as some
> understand slowness. Instead he is patient with you.
>
> 2 PETER 3:9

Dear God,

I pray for the woman who is anxiously waiting. Lord, she

knows You hold the answers, but she is tired of being so strong.

Remind her, Father, that You will prepare her heart for every

single thing she cannot yet see. In Your Holy Name, Amen.

SHAME, GUILT, AND LOATHING ARE
THE ENEMY'S DISTRACTIONS

In the journey of faith, you will still get things wrong sometimes.

When you misunderstand.
When you chase after foolish things.
When you forget to go to God first.

But God is not waiting with a list of your mistakes.

He is simply waiting for *you*.

To turn your heart back to His love.
To steer your life back to His light.

Shame and guilt and self-loathing are the Enemy's distractions.

But forgiveness is a gift from God.

Accept it from a gracious God.
Offer it to yourself.

And try to pass along a most-important note to your heart:

You needed that grace.

The world needs it too.

> All are justified freely by his grace through the
> redemption that came by Christ Jesus.
> ROMANS 3:23–24

Dear God,

I pray for the woman who is recovering from pain she

cannot talk about. Lord, she never expected these battles,

and each day she fights wars on the inside. Remind

her, Father, that You see her struggles and You will see

her through every one. In Your Holy Name, Amen.

GOD WILL NEVER GIVE UP ON YOU

After you have fallen short.
After you have run from God.
After you have made the big mistake.

It may be impossible to believe that God is still for you.

Because you feel so deeply that you have missed the mark.
Because this is when others have abandoned you.

But God does not stay silent or idle.

He chases after you with a never-ending love.

And right before you find yourself consumed.

He forgives. He forgives. He forgives.

Today, let this truth that is so hard to accept enter your heart:

God can use it all. *Let Him.*

If we confess our sins, he is faithful and just and
will forgive us our sins and purify us.
1 JOHN 1:9

Dear God, I pray for the woman who is trying to forgive herself. Lord, no one is perfect, but she has been hard on herself. Remind her, Father, that You keep no record of wrongs, and You wait for her with open arms. In Your Holy Name, Amen.

And she stopped comparing.

God did not make her
like anyone else.

On purpose for a purpose.

And God's love set her free.

GOD DOES NOT REQUIRE OR
DESIRE YOUR PERFECTION

You just want to get it right.

To do all the right things. To say all the right things.

But the people pleaser in you is crushed when you fall short.

Not because you are a failure.
But because you are a living, breathing human.

God knows that. And He loves you anyway.

When the world makes its disapproval loud, it is a difficult truth to believe.

Which is why God created prayer.

When you miss the mark, you can run to Him.

He will take your hand.
He will calm your heart.
He will never fail to welcome you.

Not because you are perfect, but because you are fearfully and wonderfully made.

With a *perfect* love.

But perfect love drives out fear.

I JOHN 4:18

Dear God,

I pray for the woman who is questioning her worth.

Lord, she has been made to feel unloved and not

enough. Remind her, Father, that You do not measure

or compare; her heart is perfect and full of purpose

in Your eyes. In Your Holy Name, Amen.

TURN YOUR INSECURITIES OVER TO GOD

The Enemy is a liar.

And, sometimes, he is convincing:

"You are not enough."

And you might try to fight these toxic thoughts as if one day, they will magically stop.

You read the books.
You do the rituals and routines.

But nothing will change until you start to pray about the negative words that keep you up at night.

And get honest with God about every insecurity.

That is when life will begin to lighten.
That is when you can start to live in freedom again.

Today, hear this truth:

God knows the weapons.
God understands the damage.

But abundant life in Christ means He will cover you in His peace.

And never again will you have to fight your battles alone.

The Lord your God, who is going before you, will fight for you.
Deuteronomy 1:30

Dear God,

I pray for the woman who is trying hard to change things

in her life. Lord, the unhealthy cycles and challenges

have kept her from Your plan for too long. Remind

her, Father, that You will give her the grace to keep

going and growing. In Your Holy Name, Amen.

GOD NEVER GROWS WEARY OF YOUR PRAYERS

Sometimes it feels like you pray the same prayer over and over.

And a part of your pride aches that you just cannot seem to figure life out.

But remember that the journey of faith is supposed to humble you.

At God's feet, you must confess that you do not have all the answers.

At God's feet, you must accept that only He knows the *how*.

God never grows weary of your prayers or your persistent needs.

He is your Father.

He loves you without end.

And He wants to lead you to the living.

So keep running to Him.

Because He who holds tomorrow wants to hold your hand too.

Let us then approach God's throne of grace with confidence.
Hebrews 4:16

Dear God,

I pray for the woman who is waiting for You to come through.

Lord, You know her struggle and the burden that is weighing

so heavy on her heart. Remind her, Father, that You are

the Rebuilder and Restorer, and she can still trust the work

to Your miraculous hands. In Your Holy Name, Amen.

FEELINGS ARE FLEETING, BUT GOD IS FAITHFUL

When you have bad days and the sun does not seem to shine.

Faith tells you that God is still good.

When you have hard days and the healing just will not come.

Faith tells you that God is still good.

Because feelings are fleeting.

But God is the One who *stays*.

So today, accept this truth that strengthens:

God is faithful through it all.

And He wants to build your heart on His firm foundation:

Unshaking. Unwavering. Always and forever love.

> For the Word of the LORD is right and true;
> he is faithful in all he does.
>
> PSALM 33:4

Dear God, I pray for the woman who is hurting in the pain of right now. Lord, her situation is tough, and it is taking everything she has to hold on. Remind her, Father, that You built her for hard things, and she never has to endure them alone. In Your Holy Name, Amen.

*A*nd she was not
broken or damaged.

She was learning.
She was growing.

And God never stopped
pouring love into her heart.

GOD WILL BUILD YOU UP

The Enemy is absolutely relentless.

He wants you to stumble.
He wants you to fall.

Until all that is left are the shattered pieces of your life.

But God offers you a different way.

Bring your weary. Bring your broken.

I am the Healer.

And you do not need to be afraid.

Because God sees every part of who you are.

He responds with love.

And He fights to build you up in faith.

So if you feel the world pressing in, do not despair.

God is drawing you close.

And you can trust every single thing you carry to His almighty hands.

He gives strength to the weary and increases the power of the weak.
ISAIAH 40:28–29

Dear God,

I pray for the woman who is still standing. Lord, she has been

through the hardest of life, but still her soul is anchored to

You. Remind her, Father, that when her strength fails, You

will keep her eyes lifted to You. In Your Holy Name, Amen.

day 50

GOD CAN BREAK THE CHAINS OF PERFECTION

The world wants shiny and flawless.

And there is a part of you that wants that too.

So you listen to the voices.

And you shop.
And you spend.

And you try to make yourself fit into a box that God did not design.

But your efforts never leave you full or fulfilled.

Only empty and yearning for more.

But when you trust that God has a different plan for you, He does more than simply strengthen you.

He breaks every chain holding your heart hostage:

In Me, there is freedom. In Me, there is forever hope.

And the desire for perfection is replaced with His perfect peace.

> He brought them out of darkness, the utter
> darkness, and broke away their chains.
> PSALM 107:14

Dear God,

I pray for the woman who feels like she is constantly failing.

Lord, no matter how hard she tries or how hopeful she is, she

cannot seem to get things right. Remind her, Father, that every

single day with You is new, and Your love keeps no record; it

believes in her every moment. In Your Holy Name, Amen.

YOU WILL NEVER FIND PEACE IN COMPARISON

You are harder on yourself than anyone else is.

And it trickles into your faith.

When you feel unworthy.
When you feel undeserving.

And when you feel like everyone else has it together.

Life is not meant to be spent in comparison, but in compassion for yourself and others.

God does not expect perfect.

So let it go.

Because peace is not a feeling but a humble knowing that God is near you.

In every step and stumble along the way.

> But seek first his kingdom and his righteousness, and
> all these things will be given to you as well.
> MATTHEW 6:33

Dear God, I pray for the woman who is trying to find her path. Lord, she thought she was there before, but Your peace never came to her heart. Remind her, Father, that You understand her unique purpose, and You will straighten her steps with every promise. In Your Holy Name, Amen.

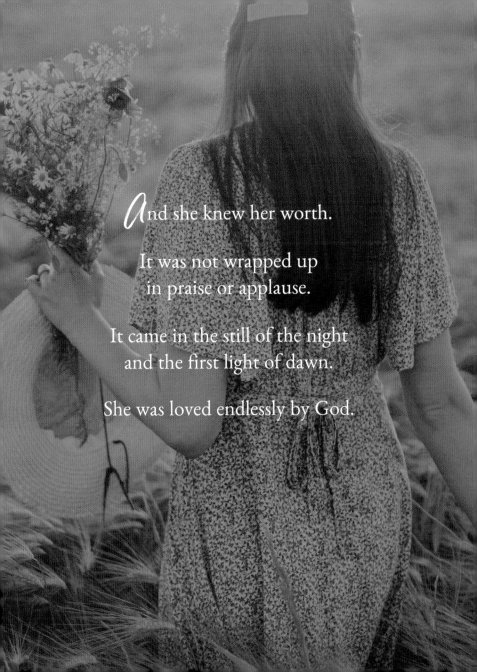

And she knew her worth.

It was not wrapped up
in praise or applause.

It came in the still of the night
and the first light of dawn.

She was loved endlessly by God.

WALK HUMBLY WITH GOD

The world wants you to buy into the good life.

The glimmering house.
The shiny résumé.
The golden relationship.

The truth is, none of that protects you when the hardest of life hits.

But God can. But God will.

And He calls you with the most gentle and loving invitation:

Walk humbly with Me.

I, the Lord, will give you rest.
I, the Lord, will bring you comfort.
I, the Lord, will carry you to hope.

You cannot surrender your life to Him without surrendering your stuff.

Today, lay it all down at His feet.

And embrace a simpler story.

One that does not overstuff your soul.

But finally, *finally* gives it a chance to breathe.

> For we brought nothing into the world, and
> we can take nothing out of it.
> 1 TIMOTHY 6:6–7

Dear God,

I pray for the woman who wants a simpler life. Lord,

she remembers when she found joy in the small things,

and she wants that again for her heart. Remind her,

Father, that You will lead her to what is important—

that You will never stop guiding her to an abundant

and whole life. In Your Holy Name, Amen.

BUT GOD KNOWS YOU

People will form opinions of you, and none of them may be true.

But God knows you.

Circumstances may stress and suck the life out of you.

But God knows you.

Relationships you thought would last forever may crumble.

But God knows you.

Today, no matter the giant you face, let that be enough.

God understands the longing of your heart.
God honors every act of devoted faith and love.

And God is preparing you for every good thing.

The world is full of hype and half-truths.

But God is full of hope.

Live that peace.

Live that *healing* truth.

You have searched me, LORD, and you know me.
PSALM 139:1

Dear God,

I pray for the woman who is getting stronger every

day. Lord, she has given it all to You, and she feels

You rebuilding her life. Remind her, Father, that

small steps with big faith will sustain her soul through

every storm. In Your Holy Name, Amen.

GOD KNEW THE WORLD NEEDED A "YOU"

In the seasons of struggle, it is impossible to see it.

God made you on purpose for a purpose.

As He was designing His perfect creation, you came to mind.

And despite everything this world tells you, you were crafted in His holy image.

God knew the world needed a "you."

Whether you find yourself in the trial or on the mountaintop, hear these words:

God knew that you would shine a light into someone's darkness.

Live out that purpose.

God will show you how a little more every day.

> Let your light shine before others, that they may see your
> good deeds and glorify your Father in heaven.
> MATTHEW 5:16

Dear God,

I pray for the woman who is making gains that no one

else can see. Lord, she has been keeping her prayers and

hands lifted, and her growth has changed all of her life.

Remind her, Father, that You see the love in her heart and

the light she now shines. In Your Holy Name, Amen.

HOPE &

PROMISE

GOD CAN USE TODAY TO CHANGE YOUR LIFE

God is in the business of transformation.

And He never stops leading you there.

He wants to renew your life.
He wants to resurrect your heart.

And He stands ready to do the impossible every day.

When life is good, praise Him.
When life is hard, praise Him.

He knows what needs to go and what needs to stay.

He knows what will grow your faith and what will stop it in its tracks.

And you need Him every step of the way.

Trust that God is perfectly timing your transformation.

And wait for Him with an open heart.

His way is working.

His plan is perfect.

> And we all . . . are being transformed into his image with ever-increasing glory, which comes from the Lord, who is the Spirit.
>
> 2 CORINTHIANS 3:18

Dear God,

I pray for the woman who is ready to begin a new path.

Lord, she knows she will never be fully prepared, but

her heart believes this is what comes next. Remind her,

Father, that You will walk beside her through every

challenge and every change. In Your Holy Name, Amen.

GOD IS WORTHY OF YOUR TRUST

You struggle with trust.

Because people have let you down.
Because people have broken your heart.

But in His way that transcends understanding.

God will show you that He is different.

He always believes in you.
He always fights for you.

And His love is steadfast and true.

But it is up to you to follow Him.

Only you can take those steps.
Only you can make that leap.

So let this prayer linger on your lips:

"God, give me the strength."

You can trust that He leads.

You can trust *where* He leads.

Commit your way to the LORD; trust in him.

PSALM 37:5

Dear God,

I pray for the woman who is taking a leap of faith. Lord, she

is doing a brave thing she has never done because You have

called her there. Remind her, Father, that You will guide

her feet and bless every step. In Your Holy Name, Amen.

GOD WILL EQUIP YOU WITH
THE PATH AND THE PEACE

There is no light switch with God.

He will not give you everything you want.

And He will not magically turn bad things to good.

But He will equip you with the path and graciously fill you with the peace you need to walk it.

You will not be free of frustration.
You will not be free of challenge.

But you will have the greatest Advocate in your corner.

No matter what giant you face.

Today, trust in God's way with the kind of faith that says:

I am being led.
I am being loved.

And God equips me so that I can truly live.

> Now may the God of peace . . . equip you with
> everything good for doing his will.
> HEBREWS 13:20–21

Dear God,

I pray for the woman who is standing before a giant.

Lord, she has faced many challenges, but none like

this one. Remind her, Father, that in You there is

power, and by You she will be prepared. Lead her

heart to victory. In Your Holy Name, Amen.

GOD KNOWS WHAT TOMORROW WILL BRING

One day you will look back and see that God was with you.

In the messy. In the magical.

And every hard day in between.

Carving out your purpose. Sharpening your strength.

So the dark that became light could be shared.

Truly, this is the fruit of faith:

To boldly believe that God is there.
To obediently follow His lead.

And to wholly trust Him with the *why*.

Because in making all things new, God never abandons His promises.

He is making you brand-new too.

> By faith Noah, when warned about things not yet
> seen, in holy fear built an ark to save his family.
> HEBREWS 11:7

Dear God, I pray for the woman who is leaning on You. Lord, her situation is fragile, and things she thought would last forever have fallen apart. Remind her, Father, that You will keep her head lifted and that Your love is steadfast for always. In Your Holy Name, Amen.

And she trusted
her battles to God.

He knew her enemies.
He knew her heart.

And He strengthened
her to face the day.

GOD WILL MEET THE ENEMY AT THE DOOR

The closer you get to God, the greater the Enemy attacks.

And the Enemy does not always work on his own.

Sometimes he works through people in your midst.

It may catch you by surprise.
Or be a challenge you can anticipate.

But the Enemy sees nothing more dangerous than a soul on fire for God.

So run to God in prayer.

And ask for His insight and holy intervention:

"God, every battle is Yours."

When you can take a step back, you will see that God is already at the door.

Trust that God can and will handle the conflict that comes.

Because though the Enemy may arrive:

God is with you.
God is for you.

And He will never let the evil stay.

> "Do not be afraid of them, for I am with you and
> will rescue you," declares the LORD.
>
> JEREMIAH 1:8

Dear God,

I pray for the woman who feels the storm surrounding

her. Lord, she is anxious for what comes next because

it can so easily destroy. Remind her, Father, that

You will protect and provide until her heart knows

calm again. In Your Holy Name, Amen.

GOD WHISPERS, "I AM HERE"

Being a Christian means acquainting yourself with fear.

Facing it.

And trusting God in the midst of it.

Because the truth is, fear's message is simple:

"Stop. Be idle. Let your life go unused."

This constructs a barrier to not only your faith.

But your path to God Himself.

So in the midst of paralyzing fear, lean on His promise:

I am here.

And God will drop the rope.

In this world, something will always try to steal your peace.

But God is the Rescuer.

And only He can lead you to the fullest life.

One that transcends every fear.
One that turns your trials into faith.

> I sought the LORD, and he answered me; he
> delivered me from all my fears.
>
> PSALM 34:4

Dear God,

I pray for the woman who is afraid to move. Lord, she has

heard Your voice and knows hard things are ahead, but her

feet stay paralyzed. Remind her, Father, that Your strength

will steady her heart, and Your peace will lead her to her

purpose—one prayer at a time. In Your Holy Name, Amen.

PRAY YOUR WAY THROUGH

When you feel stuck and in a holding pattern, giving up looks more and more desirable.

But if you do not surrender hope.

If you do not abandon your faith.

God prepares your heart for every good thing to come.

As you feel the walls close in, lean on the promises of God:

Your life has purpose.
Your life has meaning.

And His Light will find you.

Pray your way through.

Because waiting is the most fertile soil for growth.

When everything is uncertain.
When everything feels unstable.

God remains *unchanging*.

Rich in love.

Overflowing with mercy.

> Be joyful in hope, patient in affliction, faithful in prayer.
> ROMANS 12:12

Dear God,

I pray for the woman who does not know what comes next.

Lord, she is scared and excited and unsure—all at the same

time. Remind her, Father, that You hold her tomorrow and

her heart with both hands. In Your Holy Name, Amen.

GOD WILL GIVE YOU WHAT YOU NEED

It is not easy to trust that God holds it all.

The words you need during times of conflict.
The solutions you need during times of struggle.
The hope you need when life gets heavy.

But God withholds no good thing from His children.

He marches alongside you.

And before you. And behind you.

Especially when you need that holy and healthy nudge.

And He will equip you for every challenge on the road ahead.

Today, you do not have to toil to get the life you want.

Boldly trust that God is leading you to it.

For His love will never leave you without a way.

The LORD is my strength and my defense.
PSALM 118:14

Dear God, I pray for the woman who needs You to keep going. Lord, You have blessed her with vision and passion, but she cannot arrive at Your destination unless You walk with her every step. Remind her, Father, of Your endless presence and promise of strength. In Your Holy Name, Amen.

And she believed that
God could change it all.

Her circumstances.
Her story.
Her heart.

And she followed Him
in all the days ahead.

GOD'S TIME IS DIFFERENT

The times when you are most impatient are the times when it is hardest to trust.

Because you feel like you have been holding on for so long.

You are tired and wonder what all the time and energy has been for.

And your defeated prayer is this:

"Lord, it does not feel like I will ever get there."

But God does not hear just your sorrow-filled truth.

He hears your heart cracking too.

And His words will be a balm to your soul:

My time is different. Trust. I love you.

Remember that faith is still working.

Even in your exhaustion.
Even in your "ready to give up" moments.

So when the life you are trying to build gets heavy, fall into His arms.

Let Him squeeze you close.

And rise with assurance that His love is making a way.

I am making a way in the wilderness.
ISAIAH 43:19

Dear God,

I pray for the woman who is wondering why it is

taking so long. Lord, she has tried to be faithful in

where You are calling, but her heart is tired. Remind

her, Father, that Your timing is never late and is

always perfect. In Your Holy Name, Amen.

day 64

ONLY GOD KNOWS THE DIRECTIONS

The world never leads you to the places you need to go.

And yet sometimes you wander.

Because it feels good to think you are in control.
Because it feels good to think you have some certainty.

But those feelings never, ever last.

Only God knows the directions.

Because only God knows the destination.

And you can find your way to peace as you pray:

"It is all Yours, God. Help me give it to You."

Slowly releasing what was never yours.

Because in a world that rejects more than it repents, you need God's love.

To carry you back to hope.

To build you back to *whole*.

> Lift up your eyes and look to the heavens: Who created
> all these? He who brings out the starry host one by
> one and calls forth each of them by name.
> ISAIAH 40:26

Dear God,

I pray for the woman who is waiting for the right door

to open. Lord, she is grateful to be where she is, but she

knows her heart was made for more. Remind her, Father,

that she can be confident in the future Your mighty

hands are creating. In Your Holy Name, Amen.

LOOK FOR THE GOODNESS OF GOD

If you believe that the world is terrible and full of evil, then that is what you will see.

But if you believe that God is love and the world is full of His goodness, then that is all you will see.

It takes practice when you are in the worst of life.

To pray when you do not want to.

To choose hope when you want to let go.

But God always, always meets you there:

You are loved. You are valued.

And I, the Lord, have a plan.

Today, let these words lift your soul:

You cannot miss what God has for you.

Because God is in all things.

Never stop praying for eyes that can see it.

Taste and see that the LORD is good.

PSALM 34:8

Dear God,

I pray for the woman who does not know where You

are leading her. Lord, she is trying to be obedient, but

her head is full of questions. Remind her, Father, that

You will help her find meaning in the mess and peace

for her restless thoughts. In Your Holy Name, Amen.

PRAYER HELPS YOU STAY PRESENT

It is difficult to focus on right now.

Your mind goes to the to-dos.
Your heart gets pulled to the stressors.

And you are not really present at all.

But prayer is how you find your way back.

And as soon as you begin that sacred communion with God,
He carries you with both hands:

In Me, there is no worry.
In Me, there is strength for the day.
In Me, there is life.

So today, whisper this healing truth to your heart:

When you can be present, you will be filled with God's presence.

And prayer opens the door to His abundance every time.

Look to the LORD and his strength; seek his face always.
1 CHRONICLES 16:11

Dear God, I pray for the woman who is taking on so much. Lord, her plate is full, and still more is being added. Remind her, Father, that no load is too heavy and no weight is too great for Your able and loving arms. In Your Holy Name, Amen.

And even on the hard days.

She prayed.

God would restore her peace.

God would resurrect her hope.

IN THE BROKEN MOMENTS,
GOD WILL BREAK THROUGH

Maybe you used to think you could work hard and skate across life without cracking the surface.

As if perfection was a healthy and attainable goal.

But in those golden moments where things go your way, you can miss God completely.

Believing life is about your effort and your own strength.

Until, that is, you inevitably break through the ice.

And then, you remember your Savior.

He knows how hard you try.
He knows how deeply you love.

But He also knows the world is so broken.

In the midst of your sorrow and pain, remember this promise:

God will break through.

To heal what is broken.

To bring Himself to you.

Heal me, LORD, and I will be healed; save me and I will be saved.
JEREMIAH 17:14

Dear God,

I pray for the woman who is trying to find meaning.

Lord, the problems and pain have made life and

her vision messy, but she stills sees You. Remind her,

Father, that she can trust in the timing of Your miracles

and in Your mercy. In Your Holy Name, Amen.

GOD HAS NEVER STOPPED LEADING YOU TO LIGHT

You forget the way sometimes.

Not because God forgot to lead you.

But because you get distracted by what you think is true and what everyone else is telling you.

You may even imagine that God just gets exhausted with you.

But you can find your way in the praying:

"God, help me see the way forward."

Because you may have trouble with trusting.
Because your humanness may make you forget.

He does not just hold the light.

He *is* the Light.

And His response to your prayer is the most humbling of all:

I have never stopped leading you.

Pray for eyes and ears that do not just respond.

But believe that God is who He says He is.

The only One who can lead you to true and everlasting life.

A person's steps are directed by the LORD.
PROVERBS 20:24

Dear God,

I pray for the woman who is keeping her head up. Lord, the

struggles have strained her heart, but she is not giving in.

Remind her, Father, that You will lead her to abundant

life and rich opportunities that use her beautiful gifts

and special strengths. In Your Holy Name, Amen.

THERE ARE BRIGHT AND BEAUTIFUL DAYS AHEAD

From the pit, it is impossible to see:

God is preparing.

Your eyes just do not have the strength to look up.

But faith offers a whisper: *Hold on a little longer.*

This is not the end. This is not where God is leaving you.

And you can pray for the kind of belief that keeps your feet trusting.

Because the way out is always by following God's steps alone.

And no matter how long it takes.

Do not stop.

The sleepless nights and the broken terrain are not without purpose.

They are the way to God's promises.

> Even though I walk through the darkest valley,
> I will fear no evil, for you are with me.
> PSALM 23:4

Dear God, I pray for the woman who is worn and weary. Lord, the fight has been painful, and she has forgotten her strength. Remind her, Father, that You will help her endure every impossible moment, and she can rest against Your faithful promises. In Your Holy Name, Amen.

And she found herself
facing a mountain.

She did not know how
she would climb.

She did not know how
she would endure.

But God would give
her what she needed.

One prayer at a time.

NO PRAYER IS WASTED BY GOD

Prayer does not always feel good.

And the messier your life feels, the more you worry that your words will be wasted.

But learn to pray anyway.

Because in the waiting, God is working.

In the silence, God is strengthening.

And in every heartache, God is healing.

You may not see or feel His power yet.

But it is going to lead you.

And God will lift your heart.

Because prayer is more than the words you utter in desperation.

It is how you begin.
It is how you grow.

It is how you know God loves you without end.

> If we ask anything according to his will, he hears us.
> 1 JOHN 5:14

Dear God,

I pray for the woman who wonders if You hear her

prayers. Lord, her heart has endured so much, and her

tears and fears feel unanswered. Remind her, Father,

that in silence You strengthen, and in darkness Your

light will lead her faith. In Your Holy Name, Amen.

WITH GOD, IT IS POSSIBLE

Lately, God has been growing your faith muscles.

You have faced the most impossible tasks.

Relying solely on the power and promise of prayer to get you there.

And truthfully, this has been the inner desperation on your lips:

"God, it is too hard and overwhelming."

But God never leaves you there.

He meets your weakness with strength:

With Me, it is possible.

For it is in the desert and wilderness that you can learn to discern His voice.

God made you for this moment.
God made you for more than what your eyes can see.

It is supposed to feel hard.

Nothing in faith will be easy.

But in the Father, amazing things will happen.

> With God all things are possible.
> MATTHEW 19:26

Dear God,

I pray for the woman who feels like the mountain cannot

be moved. Lord, she has prayed for change for so long

that it feels impossible. Remind her, Father, that behind

the scenes You are working and Your strength alone will

carry her to the other side. In Your Holy Name, Amen.

GOD'S GRACE WILL CARRY YOU

When you cannot see the other side.
When you do not know how you will make it.

You tend to cling to what you have.

Often, extremely tightly.

Because the trust it takes to leave the boat and walk on water.

Feels beyond you.

So you embrace excuses and continue toxic cycles.

But God, He calls you to a brighter path.

One that believes in second chances.
One that believes in forgiveness.
One that believes in healing.

And it is not just a one-time offering.

But every day.

Every hour.

God's grace will carry you where you need to be.

You can trust where He is leading.

For the LORD your God will be with you wherever you go.
JOSHUA 1:9

Dear God,

I pray for the woman who is finally making the hard and

healthy decisions. Lord, the path ahead will be full of

challenges, so she is leaning wholly on You. Remind her,

Father, that You will be her steadfast Rock as her faith

grows her to new heights. In Your Holy Name, Amen.

PART THREE

When the Future Is Faith-Filled

DEAR SISTER,

Thank you for trusting me on your journey to becoming whole.

God has special plans for your life, and He has already planted seeds of worth and wisdom in your heart. As you grow in the splendor of God's light and love, I hope you feel your faith gaining strength every day.

This does not mean the days ahead will be free of pain. But God has equipped You with eyes to see and ears to hear where He is leading. You will never venture through life's challenges alone because God does not just guide you to your purpose. He also gives you His peace.

You do not have to do what you have always done. You do not have to live as you have always lived. Instead, you can trust in God's healing to break the chains that hold you back from a fearless and faithful life. His beautiful future for you awaits.

I pray you will step into this calling in the pages ahead and in every single day to come.

I am cheering for you.

Big hugs,

Lauren

HEALING &

PEACE

FAITH DOES NOT PREVENT YOUR PROBLEMS

Following God does not prevent the bumps and bruises in life.

But it does protect you when they come.

Because faith helps reset your heart to your life's larger purpose.

The one God has spoken into your soul.

There will be hurt and loss.
But there will also be joy and love.

God promises both if you can endure.

And you will never walk alone.

In your darkest night, He is with you.
In your deepest valley, He is with you.

No matter what you face, God has not surrendered His authority.

He is still in control.
He is still leading you to the fountain of His grace.

Where peace in Him is always free.

And never, ever stops flowing.

> My unfailing love for you will not be shaken
> nor my covenant of peace be removed.
> ISAIAH 54:10

Dear God,

I pray for the woman who wants to know the path

forward. Lord, she is focused on how to get there and

desperately wants her steps to follow Yours. Remind her,

Father, that You hear every question and concern, and

You will answer every one. In Your Holy Name, Amen.

GOD NEVER PROMISED PEACE ON THE OUTSIDE

Perhaps you used to think that clinging to Jesus meant permanently escaping troubles in life.

As if, miraculously, the seas would calm and the sun would forever shine on your days.

But even Jesus could not escape the troubles and threatening conditions on earth.

There will be hurt and anguish and loss.

But you can have peace on the *inside*.

That is the hope God offers.

No matter what, you can pray.

And praise.
And prepare your heart for every hard thing.

Because God is always listening and always loving.

And you are fully known.

This is your peace.
This is your strength for enduring.
This is your roadmap to your very best life.

> I have told you these things, so that in me you may have peace.
> JOHN 16:33

Dear God,

I pray for the woman wrestling with heavy questions.

Lord, the situation is tough, and she just wants it all to

make sense. Remind her, Father, that when she walks

with You, the meaning will come—in Your way, in

Your time, in Your love. In Your Holy Name, Amen.

THE HEALING COMES WHEN YOU GIVE IT TO GOD

You tried to tuck it away and hide it.

The terrible pain.

Hoping that if you ignored the wound and did not bother anyone else with it.

You would magically heal.

But, the truth is, avoidance and denial only make the hurt grow.

And one day the burden became more than you could bear.

So you asked the only One who walks with you to save you:

"God, I need You."

And He did not just bring help.

He carried the healing too.

And every day He adds more of it to your life.

Today, let your heart carry these truths that can free you from every ache:

God's healing is not just for one time or one circumstance.
God's healing never stops.

So let Him bear your burdens this day.

> Praise be to the Lord . . . who daily bears our burdens.
> PSALM 68:19–20

Dear God,

I pray for the woman who is heading in a new direction.

Lord, she has never traveled this way before, and

sometimes she wants to turn back. Remind her, Father,

that You will lead her forward and never let her lose

sight of Your plan. In Your Holy Name, Amen.

PRAY FOR THEM ANYWAY

People will disappoint and discourage you.

Pray for them anyway.

People will hurt you and hold you back.

Pray for them anyway.

People will criticize and crush your spirit.

Pray for them anyway.

Because the pain they give you comes from their wounds.

Loving your neighbor is not about you fixing their troubles.

It is about extending grace to pray for them anyway.

Because prayer is how we tell God:

"I trust You with it all. Help my heart heal. God, the battle is Yours."

And pray in the Spirit on all occasions.
EPHESIANS 6:18

Dear God, I pray for the woman who is struggling to forgive. Lord, she knows what should have happened, but it did not. Remind her, Father, that she does not carry her pain alone and that You will heal every broken piece she places in Your hands. In Your Holy Name, Amen.

And she learned to walk
away from the things
not meant for her.

God spoke to her
through prayer.

God strengthened her
with His power.

GOD WILL LEAD YOU TO
HEALTHY AND HOLY PLACES

The closer you walk with God, the more you can rest in this promise:

God will lead you.

Not to the places you want.

But to the places where you will heal.

In His way.
In His time.

By His mighty power.

And it may not be where you expect.

Because only God can see your entire heart.
Because only God can see where you hurt most.

But none of it matters if you do not trust the Healer.

Today, lean into the One with the map and the directions.

And let Him soothe every ache with a love that says:

There are brighter days ahead that you cannot yet see.

> Turn your ear to my words. Do not let them out of your
> sight, keep them within your heart; for they are life to
> those who find them and health to one's whole body.
> PROVERBS 4:20–22

Dear God,

I pray for the woman who worries that things will

never change. Lord, she has worked tirelessly for a better

life, but the challenges just keep coming. Remind her,

Father, that You do not grow weary of loving her or

leading her with grace. In Your Holy Name, Amen.

YOU CANNOT GO BACK, BUT
GOD WILL MOVE YOU FORWARD

Sometimes, you find yourself longing for what once was.

Remembering, of course, only the good things.

And you find yourself, again, asking God:

"Why couldn't it stay that way? Why did it have to end?"

Your heart aches as it remembers the pain of change.

And in these moments, God lets you feel the hurt.

But then He offers you His strength:

I have overcome. You will too.

And you faithfully and fearlessly take the step forward.

Because it is not about how you feel.
But about what God wants to heal.

And you surrender it fully with this hope:

God wants to use what you go through to grow you.

Keep holding His hand all the way.

> Do not fear, little flock, for your Father is
> pleased to give you the kingdom.
> LUKE 12:32

Dear God,

I pray for the woman who is wondering when her heart will heal. Lord, so much time has passed, but the hurt still feels fresh and fragile. Remind her, Father, that when she needs to run from the pain, she can run into Your arms. Keep them open for every ache. In Your Holy Name, Amen.

WHERE GOD IS LEADING YOU IS BETTER

You do not always like what God gives you.

Most often, His gifts create more questions than answers.

And it is really tempting to lose a little faith in His process.

Because your head tells you that you know best.

But you can confess every uncertainty to God:

"God, I am confused."
"God, I am scared."
"God, help me find the way to You."

And, without fail, His peace will whisper:

Keep going. I, the Lord, go with you.

And this new path.

Is not broken.

But blessed.

No good thing does he withhold from those whose walk is blameless.
PSALM 84:11

Dear God,

I pray for the woman who is refusing to settle. Lord,

the world tempts her to give in at every turn, but she is

clinging tightly to Your hope. Remind her, Father, that

You will fill her with peace in the waiting and You will

grow her heart in the hard. In Your Holy Name, Amen.

GOD WILL HELP YOU DO THE
HOLY AND HEALING WORK

You used to try so hard to do the work yourself.

Grind, grind, grind. Hustle, hustle, hustle.

You kept silent all the battles you were fighting.

Because you thought you could do it alone.
Because you thought you had to carry it alone.

But God invites you to bring every burden and bad day to Him.

He is equipped for the hard.

And He knows every step of the holy and healing way.

So today, do not let the adversity and attitudes of this world enter in.

God will help you. God will hold you.

And God will make you whole when you walk it all with Him.

The LORD makes firm the steps of the one who delights in him.
PSALM 37:23

Dear God, I pray for the woman who wants to live a better story. Lord, she has God-sized goals and dreams, and she is not sure how to achieve them. Remind her, Father, that You will give her the strength to be persistent and patient in prayerful progress. In Your Holy Name, Amen.

And one day, she
stopped asking God,
"Why?"

And started asking
Him, "How?"

And with every
prayer, her purpose
became more clear.

YOU WILL DO IT WITH GOD

No matter how many times God has come through for you, doubt still finds its way in.

When you are tired.
When you have been tossed about in the seas of life.

But God always gives you the strength to pray.

Even when your words are few.
Even when your confessions are emotional.

Talk to God.

He listens.

And He whispers:

With Me. You will do it with Me.

And the impossible becomes possible.
And the mountains get moved.

In God's way.
In God's timing.

Not because of how hard you tried.

But because of how much you *trusted*.

Don't be afraid; just believe.
MARK 5:36

176

Dear God,

I pray for the woman who needs Your strength to do the next

thing. Lord, she is following You in faith, and she knows

that only Your hand can lift her over the mountains. Remind

her, Father, that she can rest in Your knowing, and You

will fuel her divine purpose. In Your Holy Name, Amen.

YOU WILL NEVER REGRET GOD'S WAY

It can take a lifetime to surrender your plans.

But if you learn to turn them over to God, here is the truth:

You will not waste time looking back.

Because this is the only way you move forward.

Toward the healthy.
Toward the healing.
Toward the whole.

God is right there to teach you how to praise in the midst of your problems.

To find strength in the midst of your struggles.

Because God's way leads you away from the endless cycles.

To depths of love your heart has never known.

But you cannot unlock this path until you trust that God holds the key.

In God there is life.

And He will equip you to endure.

Give me your heart and let your eyes delight in my ways.
PROVERBS 23:26

Dear God,

I pray for the woman who is trying to do the right

thing. Lord, she knows it will not be easy and she may

be alone, but she is trusting You. Remind her, Father,

that You are on the other side, and Your love will never

stop calling her there. In Your Holy Name, Amen.

WITHOUT THE HARD, THERE IS
NO ROOM FOR THE HOLY

It used to feel like God had placed a target on your back.

Because there were seasons when all you felt was pain.

And you could not understand how God's love could allow such hurt.

But what you could not see was this:

God was making room in your life for His glory and grace.

They do not just magically appear in the midst of comfort and wealth
and happiness.

They come through the challenging circumstances that draw you
to Him.

Where God can redeem.
Where God can rescue.

Because only God can restore your heart.

God made you for *more*.

And when you trust Him with every ache.

You get closer to the holy plan He designed just for you.

> Our present sufferings are not worth comparing
> with the glory that will be revealed in us.
> ROMANS 8:18

Dear God,

I pray for the woman who is living in ways she never

thought she could. Lord, it takes all of her strength,

but she knows You are holding her up. Remind her,

Father, that You will see her through, and Your

will leads to life. In Your Holy Name, Amen.

FAITH CHASES AWAY THE FEAR

Nothing you face is a surprise to God.

He knows your struggles. He knows your enemies.

And He knows what keeps you up at night.

God does not want the hard to steal your hope.

He wants the fear to grow your faith into action.

So that you can climb the mountain.
So that you can praise Him at the summit.

In this unique preparation, God will remind your heart:

I made you for brighter days. Keep going.

And the faith you build today.

Will chase every fear in tomorrow.

> So we say with confidence, "The Lord is my helper; I will
> not be afraid. What can mere mortals do to me?"
> HEBREWS 13:6

Dear God, I pray for the woman who is afraid to trust that good things are coming. Lord, she has had her hope crushed before, and she is struggling to believe this time will be different. Remind her, Father, that You break the chains and the cycles—that You are leading her to light. In Your Holy Name, Amen.

And she stopped letting the world determine her worth.

She did not need their applause or approval.

She was God's treasure.

And she lived for Him.

LOVE CHANGES YOUR HEART

You cannot change other people.

No matter how hard you try.
No matter how hard you pray.

But God gives you the gift of grace.

And you can choose to love them.

Even when they hurt you.
Even when they disappoint you.

Love is a holy invitation from God to grow.

And every single person and circumstance can build your faith and trust in Him.

There will be pain and heartbreak in this life.

But when you live more like Jesus, you unlock the way to peace.

You do not have to give the world a piece of your mind.

When you give God all of your heart.

> I will give them an undivided heart and put a new
> spirit in them; I will remove from them their heart
> of stone and give them a heart of flesh.
> EZEKIEL 11:19

Dear God,

I pray for the woman who wants to make peace with

the past. Lord, forgiveness has not been easy, but she is

trying to offer grace every day. Remind her, Father, that

when her heart cannot give any more, You will keep her

light shining with love. In Your Holy Name, Amen.

A PERFECT SAVIOR DOES NOT
DEMAND YOUR PERFECTION

Because God is perfect, you do not have to be.

It is the reminder you need most days.

And it frees your heart every single time you remember.

You do not have to carry the weight of the world.
You do not have to carry the pressure you put on yourself.

God wants you to know that His arms and hands are able.

He can carry not only your burdens.

But your heart too.

So let this simple grace fill you with a knowing peace:

In the messes, God is there.
In the mistakes, God is there.

And in the mystery of wondering how you will survive, God is there.

He is writing a better story.

Even in this moment.

> As for God, his way is perfect: The LORD's word is
> flawless; he shields all who take refuge in him.
> PSALM 18:30

Dear God,

I pray for the woman who does not feel worthy of

Your love. Lord, You have given her countless blessings

and second chances, but she knows that she still falls

short. Remind her, Father, that the love You provide

is unending and Your promises make her strong in

every weak moment. In Your Holy Name, Amen.

THE ENEMY CANNOT KEEP YOU
FROM GOD'S DESTINATION

When you are discouraged, the Enemy's lies sound like truth:

"You are not good enough."
"You will never make it."

And you begin to wonder if God has a special plan for you after all.

But the truth is, it does not matter what you see or what you hear.

God is still in charge of the destination.

And no distraction or disturbance from the Enemy is going to deny it.

So if your heart is feeling low, guard this truth with your life:

God loves you. God is leading you.

And God's dream for you is *unwavering*.

> Neither height nor depth, nor anything else in all creation,
> will be able to separate us from the love of God.
> ROMANS 8:39

Dear God, I pray for the woman who is trying not to be crushed by discouragement. Lord, she has been working hard to walk in Your ways, but the doors keep closing. Remind her, Father, that Your hope is the key that will unlock a brighter and blessed future ahead. In Your Holy Name, Amen.

And she took the leap
of faith and trusted.

She no longer worried
about falling or failing.

Because God held her today.

And in all the days to come.

YOU WILL SEE THAT GOD DID IT OUT OF LOVE

When seemingly wonderful things go away, it is difficult not to feel like the mighty hand of God has taken them from you.

Like God is punishing you.
Like God is rejecting you.

But if you can keep the faith, the healing truth comes:

God loves you.

God is in the business of protecting your heart.

And He does not want you to waste your days wrapped up in endless questions.

God's way for you is not to always understand.
God's way for you is to trust.

And you can believe that the God who takes away out of love is the same God who will bless your life out of love too.

> The LORD gave and the LORD has taken away;
> may the name of the LORD be praised.
>
> JOB 1:21

Dear God,

I pray for the woman who cannot understand why.

Lord, she has prayed for answers and meaning, but she

cannot find peace in her heart. Remind her, Father,

that where her words end is where Your unending

grace begins. In Your Holy Name, Amen.

NOT BY YOUR STRENGTH, BUT GOD'S

Before you get out of bed, give the day to God.

Your plans and predictions will fall short.

But God's purposes are perfect.

And you will find that if you hold on to anything, it will hold you back.

So ask God to empty you.

Then pray for Him to fill you with His silent strength.

That can cut through the uncertainty.
That can crush the insecurity.

Because the battles are massive and many.

But you can trust this God who holds you.

And only His hands are mighty to save.

Ah, Sovereign LORD, you have made the heavens and the earth by your great power and outstretched arm. Nothing is too hard for you.
JEREMIAH 32:17

Dear God,

I pray for the woman who is ready to stand on her own

two feet again. Lord, she has not felt peace in a long

time, but she has found her strength in You. Remind

her, Father, that no matter what she faces ahead,

her home is in You. In Your Holy Name, Amen.

GOD IS GOOD, EVEN WHEN LIFE IS NOT

People get sick. Relationships change.
And sometimes, your greatest dreams are interrupted.

But God is good.

Jobs go away. Promises are broken.
And sometimes, your worst-case scenario manifests.

But God is good.

And you can run, walk, and crawl back to this truth through prayer.

Because only God can fix a broken heart and spirit.

Remember that in the valley of disappointment and despair is where
God calls your name and draws you close:

You are loved. You are Mine.

There are bright and beautiful days you have yet to see. Keep the faith.

I will see the goodness of the LORD in the land of the living.
PSALM 27:13

Dear God, I pray for the woman whose heart is slowly healing. Lord, she has been giving herself space to feel and grow, but she sees how far she still has to go. Remind her, Father, that You will journey with her in every brave step forward— no matter how small. In Your Holy Name, Amen.

EPILOGUE

What comes after God transforms your life? I wish I had those answers. I wish I could tell you that it only gets easier from here. And I wish I could tell you that healing does, in fact, have a timeline. But faith simply calls us to keep moving forward. Even when. Even if.

I know this to be true because I encountered God in a darkened closet five years ago, and I could not have imagined what came next: moving across the country with my family; journeying with my father through cancer until his very last breath; grieving in isolation during the COVID-19 lockdowns; pausing my teaching career to solely write; and creating a global Sisterhood for women on my social media platforms.

A single thought brings me to my knees every single day: God can turn your trials into a testimony. But first, you must carry the heavy and hard to Him. You must leave every broken piece at His feet. And You must walk away with trust in your heart.

Your difficult season may be over, or you may find yourself still in its midst. But God has given to you this promise: "The Lord himself goes before you and will be with you; he will never leave you nor forsake you.

Do not be afraid; do not be discouraged" (Deuteronomy 31:8). God is our security when the seas rage, and He is our shelter when the storms come. But how we choose to live our lives in the "after" makes all the difference.

I pray the last ninety days have reminded you that God made you for a unique and special purpose—one that becomes clearer through prayer and spending time in His Word. Because the closer we walk with God, the easier it is to hold His precious peace and believe in the loving promises He has spoken over our lives and into our hearts. We do not have to live stressed and stretched when we rely on His strength. We do not have to feel overwhelmed and overlooked when we trust in His sovereign love.

The journey of pursuing a relationship with God will never be without challenge, but I hope these prayers and devotions have encouraged you that there is time for God in our days, and we need Him every moment. God loves you endlessly, and He will call you to more in faith.

And that future He has prepared will be so much more than enough.

It will set your heart free.

ACKNOWLEDGMENTS

This book could not have been written without my number one fan: Mom. I am thankful for how you walked me to the library, defined the big words, and carried that folded poem in your wallet all those years ago. I also cannot fully express my gratitude for my Big Sister, Kristie. Your words and love have protected me all the days of my life.

I am eternally grateful for my little ones, Jansen and Aspen. From encouraging me to share the wild stories of my life to graciously giving me moments with my phone to write, this book is possible because you two have held my hand no matter what and have laughed with me through every tear. Thank you for helping me remember how to dream in color.

I would like to thank my husband for giving me a year to write and walk the journey of cancer with my father. I am grateful for how you have kept my tummy and gas tank full during the messy process of becoming. Your love means the world to me. Let's keep climbing the mountains. I would also like to express my gratitude for an extended family that has loved me as their own: Momma Mel, Papa Cliff, Aunt Judy Ann, Uncle Bob, and Mawmaw.

Mom Mom Fix, I want to thank you for your support and strength all these years. I will never forget your face when I told you I was writing a book. I love you, and I am forever grateful for the beautiful example of marriage that you and Pop Pop showed to me.

For the amazing Sisters who have walked this journey with me, hand in hand and prayer by prayer: Brittany, Ashley, Brandy, Megan, Karen, Jessica, Lindsay, Heather, Lauren, and Amy. Thank you for loving me at my lowest and celebrating with me at my highest. Each of you has blessed my life immeasurably.

For the wonderful Sisters who have ventured with me through motherhood, grief, and faith across the digital miles over the last eight years, this book is part yours. Without you, I never would have kept writing. Without you, I never would have believed that God had greater plans for my pain. Let's keep blooming together in His love.

For the indescribable grace and leadership of my pastors over the years, I am who I am today because you poured Jesus into me. Thank you, Chip, Tommy, Todd, Pastor Bill, Pastor Bryon, and Brother Don. Also, I would like to express my gratitude for my Brother in digital ministry, Matt B. Thank you for believing so deeply in my work for the Lord.

I am forever grateful for all of the teachers who have whispered words of encouragement into my soul at exactly the right moments. Thank you for reminding me of what is possible. *Susan, I finally found the fire in my belly.*

A special thank-you to my publishing mentor and editor, Kara, Bonnie, and the entire team at HarperCollins Christian Publishing. Each of you has made this journey a joy.

I would not be the writer I am today without the hundreds of students I have taught over the years at Spotswood, Georgia Southern, Lafayette, and Ole Miss. Thank you for challenging me to grow as you grew.

Heartfelt gratitude also goes to Dr. Stephen Monroe, John T, and my DWR family at the University of Mississippi. Thank you for your excitement and your encouragement during this busy and beautiful season of life.

Finally, I would like to offer a prayer of thanksgiving to heaven, where my father waits for me. *Daddy, you were right. My ship came in.* I will forever cherish our thirty-five years together.

Thank You, Lord, most of all for the hard and the hurt and the healing. Thank You for never letting me go. Thank You for giving me the words to remind women across the world that You hold them too. For Your Son, for the Holy Spirit, for the grace that passes all understanding. You made my darkness light, and You made my heart whole. I owe it all because You paid it all to set me free.

ABOUT THE AUTHOR

Lauren Fortenberry is a writer, speaker, and influencer whose passion is fearlessly and faithfully encouraging women through the love of Jesus Christ. She is a writing instructor at the University of Mississippi, and her writing has been featured by *The TODAY Show*, *Good Morning America*, and a variety of other media outlets and blogs. She lives in Oxford, Mississippi, with her husband and two children.

laurenfortenberry.com
@laurenfortenberrywriter
@laurenfortenberrywrites
𝕏 @Lauren410berry